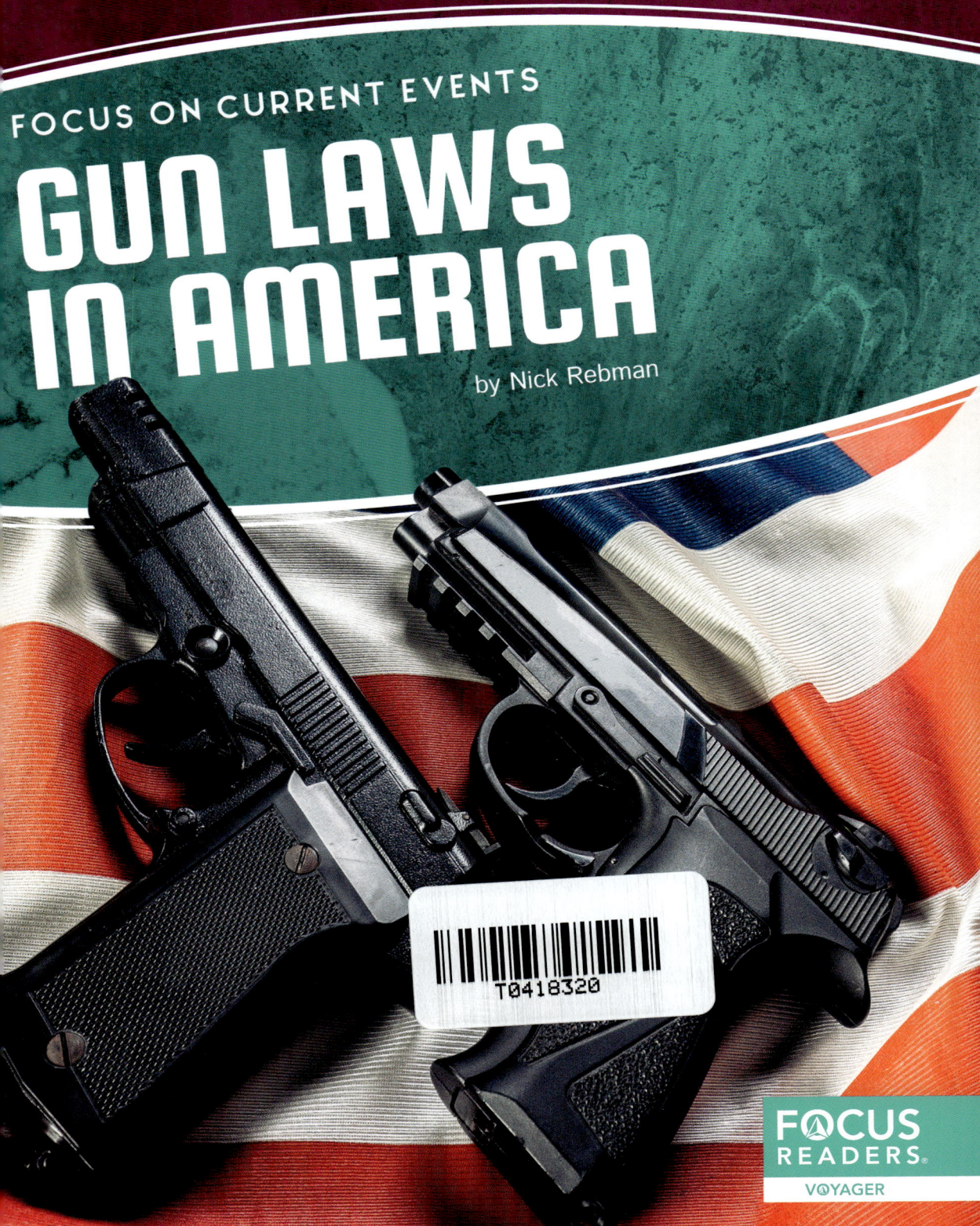

www.focusreaders.com

Copyright © 2024 by Focus Readers®, Lake Elmo, MN 55042. All rights reserved. No part of this book may be reproduced or utilized in any form or by any means without written permission from the publisher.

Focus Readers is distributed by North Star Editions:
sales@northstareditions.com | 888-417-0195

Produced for Focus Readers by Red Line Editorial.

Content Consultant: Michael Rocque, PhD, Associate Professor of Sociology, Bates College

Photographs ©: Shutterstock Images, cover, 1, 6, 13, 19, 22–23, 31, 33, 34–35, 41, 45; Joshua Bessex/AP Images, 4–5; North Wind Picture Archives/Alamy, 8–9, 10; AP Images, 14–15; Walt Zeboski/AP Images, 17; Jose Luis Magana/AP Images, 21; Patrick Semansky/AP Images, 24; Red Line Editorial, 27, 39; Allison Bailey/NurPhoto/AP Images, 28–29; Gerard Edic/The Commonwealth/AP Images, 37; iStockphoto, 42–43

Library of Congress Cataloging-in-Publication Data
Library of Congress Cataloging-in-Publication Data is available on the Library of Congress website.

ISBN
978-1-63739-640-7 (hardcover)
978-1-63739-697-1 (paperback)
978-1-63739-804-3 (ebook pdf)
978-1-63739-754-1 (hosted ebook)

Printed in the United States of America
Mankato, MN
082023

ABOUT THE AUTHOR
Nick Rebman is a writer and editor who lives in Minnesota.

TABLE OF CONTENTS

CHAPTER 1
Tragedy Leads to Change 5

CHAPTER 2
Early Gun Laws 9

CHAPTER 3
Gun Laws in the 1900s 15

CASE STUDY
District of Columbia v. Heller 20

CHAPTER 4
Gun Ownership and Gun Violence 23

CHAPTER 5
Gun-Control Debates 29

CHAPTER 6
Different Laws, Different Outcomes 35

CASE STUDY
Firearm Licenses 40

CHAPTER 7
Finding Common Ground 43

Focus on Gun Laws in America • 46
Glossary • 47
To Learn More • 48
Index • 48

CHAPTER 1

TRAGEDY LEADS TO CHANGE

On May 14, 2022, a gunman entered a grocery store in Buffalo, New York. Using a semi-automatic rifle, he killed 10 people. He injured three others. The shooting made headlines across the United States. However, the nation's shocked citizens barely had time to grieve. Ten days later, a different gunman entered a school in Uvalde, Texas. Using a semi-automatic rifle, he killed 21 people. He injured 18 others.

The Buffalo shooter had racist motives. All the people he killed were Black.

▲ Conservative and liberal lawmakers tend to disagree about the causes of gun violence.

These mass shootings set off a national debate about gun laws. The debate was nothing new, though. In the previous two decades, more than 100 mass shootings had taken place in the United States. Time after time, gun-control supporters called for stronger laws. Meanwhile, gun-control opponents argued against such laws.

Congress remained divided. So, no major gun laws were passed.

However, the shootings in Buffalo and Uvalde led to a shift in attitudes. Several **conservative** lawmakers had previously resisted stronger gun-control laws. But now they agreed to make certain changes. In June, lawmakers from both major political parties voted for the Bipartisan Safer Communities Act. President Joe Biden signed it into law.

The new law expanded **background checks** on gun buyers under the age of 21. The law also focused on people believed to be dangerous. States could more easily take firearms away from them. In addition, the law set aside money. This money was for mental health services and school safety. Biden said the law did not go far enough. Even so, he believed it would save lives.

CHAPTER 2

EARLY GUN LAWS

Gun laws have existed in America since before the United States was founded. In the 1600s, colonists followed English common law. This set of laws gave people the right to own guns for self-defense. However, colonists also created gun-control laws. For example, Virginia banned the sale of guns to Indigenous people.

Most colonies required white men to join militias. These groups were not professional

In the 1600s, many colonists used muskets. Compared to modern guns, muskets were not very accurate.

▲ The Battles of Lexington and Concord began when the British tried to take colonists' guns in 1775.

armies. Instead, they were made up of ordinary citizens. They had several purposes. Militias defended the colonies. They attacked Indigenous groups to take land. Many militias also put down revolts of enslaved Africans. Laws required militia members to own guns. That way, they would be ready to fight.

By the 1760s, tensions were growing between the colonists and the British government. Some colonists set up militias to oppose British rule. In response, the British government tried to limit the militias' access to guns. War soon broke out. The militias fought in the American Revolutionary War (1775–1783). They helped the United States gain its independence.

In 1787, US lawmakers wrote the Constitution. This document laid out the laws of the new country. Lawmakers also wrote the Bill of Rights, which took effect in 1791. The Bill of Rights is made up of 10 **amendments** to the Constitution. Each amendment lists specific rights. The Second Amendment is about militias and firearms. It reads, "A well regulated Militia, being necessary to the security of a free State, the right of the people to keep and bear Arms, shall not be infringed."[1]

1. "The Bill of Rights: A Transcription." *National Archives*. The US National Archives and Records Administration, n.d. Web. 15 Dec. 2022.

The Second Amendment did not cause much debate in the 1800s. During this period, states passed a wide variety of gun-control laws. Some laws prohibited people from carrying **concealed** guns. Other laws prohibited people from pointing guns at others. Many states passed laws that prevented Black people from owning guns. A few states banned the sale of all handguns. Some of these laws faced challenges in court. However, in nearly all cases, judges ruled that states had the right to pass gun-control laws.

Gun technology began to change in the 1800s. Firearms became much more accurate. They could

➤ THINK ABOUT IT

America's tradition of gun ownership goes back hundreds of years. Do you think this tradition is still important today? Why or why not?

▲ During the 1870s and 1880s, the sale of handguns was banned in Arkansas, Kansas, Tennessee, and Texas.

also fire several shots before being reloaded. These new weapons could cause more harm. They also became more common over time. So, in the interest of public safety, many lawmakers called for stronger gun-control laws.

CHAPTER 3

GUN LAWS IN THE 1900S

A machine gun is a fully automatic firearm. That means it keeps firing as long as the trigger is pulled. Many states banned machine guns in the late 1920s. These new laws were a response to increases in violent crime. Some states went even further. They banned semi-automatic firearms, too. This type of gun fires a single shot each time the trigger is pulled.

Gang-related violence increased during the 1920s after the United States banned the sale of alcohol.

In 1934, US lawmakers passed the National Firearms Act. The law created a heavy tax on certain kinds of firearms. These included machine guns and short-barreled shotguns. The law also required gun owners to **register** certain firearms with the government. Lawmakers hoped to make these guns too inconvenient to own.

A few years later, a man named Jack Miller was arrested. He had a short-barreled shotgun that was not registered. In 1939, his case went to the US Supreme Court. The court ruled that Miller's gun was not intended to be used in a militia. Therefore, the Second Amendment did not give Miller the right to own the gun. This decision meant the government could continue regulating guns that were not used in militias.

In the 1960s, the Black Panther Party formed in California. Its members openly carried firearms.

▲ Members of the Black Panther Party protest a 1967 gun-control law at the California State Capitol.

Their goal was to protect Black communities from racist police officers. Many conservative lawmakers saw the Black Panthers as a threat. So, in 1967, California passed a gun-control law. Open carry became illegal without a license.

The 1960s also saw several high-profile assassinations. President John F. Kennedy was killed in November 1963. Civil rights leader Martin Luther King Jr. was killed in April 1968. And Senator Robert F. Kennedy was killed in June 1968. Firearms were used in all three assassinations.

In response, Congress passed the Gun Control Act of 1968. This law required gun sellers to have a license. The law also banned the sale of guns to certain people. The list included people convicted of crimes, users of illegal drugs, and people with mental illness. However, gun sales actually increased after the law went into effect. Studies also showed that the law did not lower **homicide** rates.

In the early 1990s, **liberal** lawmakers called for additional gun-control laws. They were responding to recent mass shootings. In 1994, Congress passed the **Federal** Assault Weapons Ban. An assault weapon is a type of

▲ The 1994 Federal Assault Weapons Ban prohibited firearms that held more than 10 rounds of ammunition.

semi-automatic gun that can hold many rounds of ammunition.

Over the next decade, the United States saw a decrease in mass shootings. However, the overall rate of gun violence did not decrease. That was because the vast majority of gun violence does not involve assault weapons. Instead, most gun violence involves handguns. This fact was true even before the ban.

CASE STUDY

DISTRICT OF COLUMBIA V. HELLER

By the early 2000s, Washington, DC, had some of the strongest gun-control laws in the United States. All guns had to be registered. Guns also had to be kept unloaded or locked. In addition, handguns were banned in nearly all cases. However, people could apply for a one-year handgun license.

Police officer Dick Anthony Heller applied for a license. Washington, DC, did not give him the license. So, Heller **appealed** the decision. His case went all the way to the Supreme Court. In 2008, the court ruled in Heller's favor. The decision said DC's gun-control laws went against the Second Amendment. It said the Second Amendment is not limited to militias. Therefore, all individuals have the right to keep guns for self-defense.

▲ Dick Anthony Heller walks among gun-control supporters and opponents after the Supreme Court's 2008 ruling.

Due to this ruling, DC had to end its ban on handguns. However, the court did allow some limits. One limit involved people convicted of serious crimes. These people could still be prohibited from owning guns. Also, guns could still be banned in certain places. These locations include schools and government buildings.

CHAPTER 4

GUN OWNERSHIP AND GUN VIOLENCE

The United States is home to more guns than any other country. As of 2022, US citizens owned more than 393 million firearms. Meanwhile, the US population was 332 million. That means the United States has more guns than people.

Another way to look at these numbers is with ratios. In the United States, there are 120 guns per 100 people. This ratio is much lower in other

In 2020, gun violence was the leading cause of death for children and teenagers in the United States.

▲ Approximately 30 Black Americans die from gun violence every day. An additional 110 are injured.

developed countries. In Canada, for example, there are 35 guns per 100 people. In Germany, there are 20 per 100. And in Japan, there are 0.3 per 100.

The United States also has one of the highest rates of gun violence in the world. In 2020, the United States recorded more than 45,000 firearm deaths. That comes out to 14 deaths per 100,000 people. In the same period, Canada's rate was 2 deaths per 100,000 people. Germany's rate was 1 per 100,000. Japan's rate was 0.01 per 100,000.

Gun violence in the United States does not affect all people equally. Black Americans and low-income Americans face the highest risk. Black people make up only 14 percent of the US population. But they accounted for 62 percent of firearm homicide victims in 2020.

White Americans and high-income Americans are at relatively low risk. White people make up 62 percent of the US population. However, they accounted for only 21 percent of firearm homicide victims in 2020.

Domestic violence is also a factor in many shootings. According to federal law, people convicted of domestic violence cannot own guns. Even so, many states do not always enforce this law. As a result, abusers can often buy firearms. When that happens, the abuser's partner is four times more likely to become a victim of gun violence.

In addition, domestic violence often plays a role in mass shootings. One study found that two-thirds of mass shootings involve domestic violence. Sometimes, the shooter had a history of abuse. Other times, the shooter killed at least one family member or partner.

Mass shootings receive heavy attention from the media. However, they make up only 1 percent of all gun deaths in the United States. The vast majority of firearm homicides involve fewer than four victims. Also, homicides account for only 43 percent of gun deaths. The largest category is suicides. In 2020, for example, 54 percent of gun deaths involved people who died by suicide.

LIVES LOST

Each dot on this chart represents one human being who died of gun-related violence in 2020.

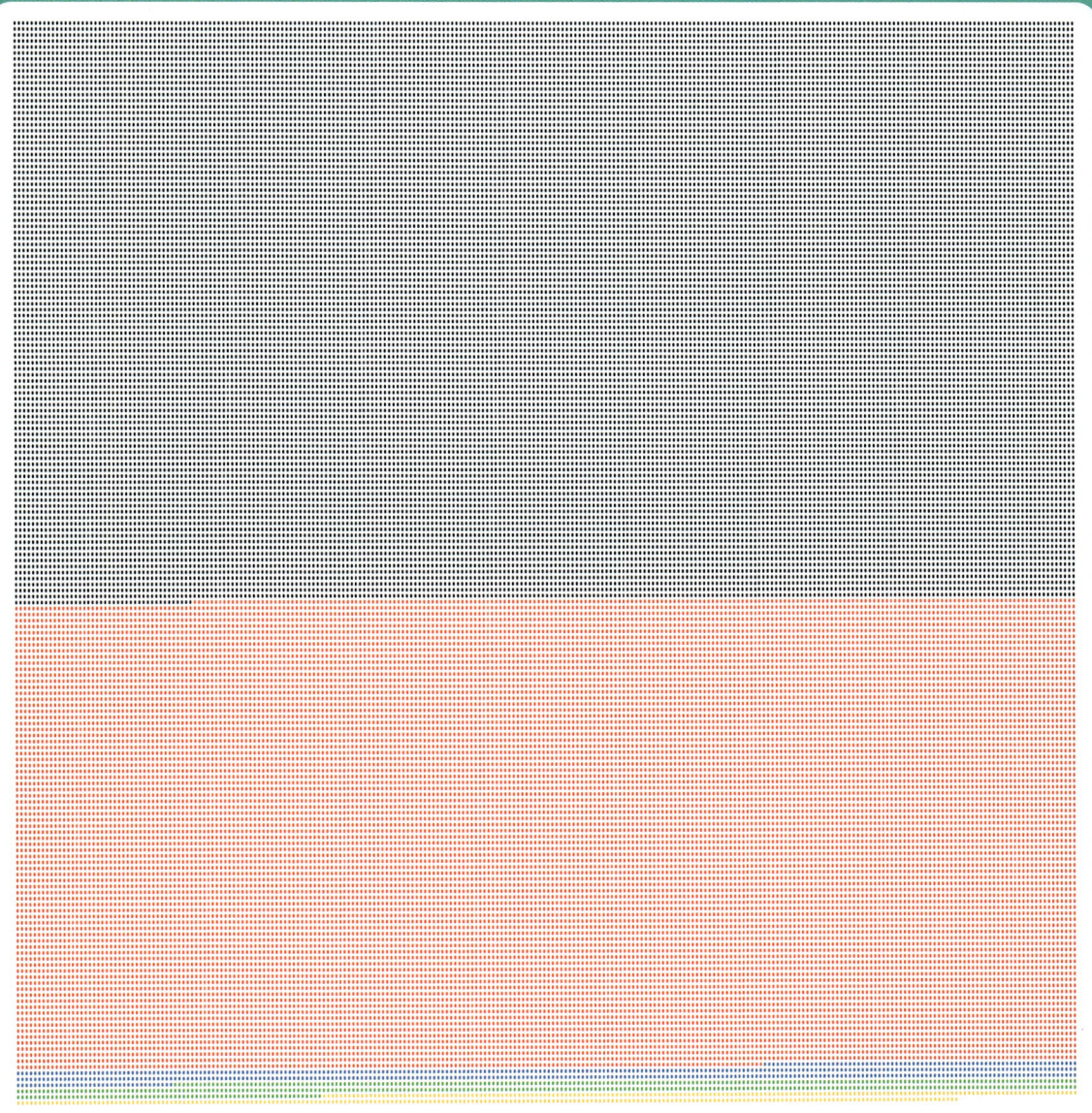

- Suicide: 24,292 people
- Homicide: 19,384 people
- Police-involved: 611 people
- Accidental: 535 people
- Unknown cause: 400 people

CHAPTER 5

GUN-CONTROL DEBATES

For decades, gun laws have led to heated debates. Gun-control opponents offer many arguments against stronger laws. For example, opponents argue that every person has the right to self-defense. They point out that firearms allow people to respond quickly to danger.

Gun-control supporters put forth a different view. They agree that people have the right to self-defense. But they argue this right is not

Some gun-control opponents want teachers to carry firearms.

applied to all Americans equally. For instance, Black people are far more likely than white people to be arrested for having firearms.

Opponents also claim that gun ownership makes crime less likely. They note that violent crime dropped by more than half between 1991 and 2019. Over the same period, gun ownership doubled.

Gun-control supporters point to studies on what caused the decrease in violent crime. These studies concluded that gun ownership played no role. Gun-control supporters also compare the United States with other countries. If guns made crime less likely, they say the United States should

➤ THINK ABOUT IT

Do you think guns make crime less likely or more likely? Why?

Many students called for stronger gun-control laws after a 2018 mass shooting in Parkland, Florida.

have the lowest crime rate in the world. But this is not the reality. The US crime rate is similar to the rates in most other developed countries.

Opponents also maintain that gun-control laws will not stop criminals from getting guns. If guns are banned or controlled, then people who follow the law will be unarmed. However, criminals will ignore the law. As a result, innocent people will be at greater risk.

Supporters agree that no law is followed by everyone. Even so, they say certain gun-control laws are highly effective. States with strong gun laws typically have low rates of firearm violence.

Individuals are not the only ones involved in the debate. Various organizations also oppose gun-control laws. Companies that make guns are one example. The National Rifle Association (NRA) is another. The NRA gives money to conservative groups and lawmakers. This **lobbying** has proven to be effective. In 2005, for instance, the NRA successfully pushed for a law that protects gun companies. Gun companies cannot be sued when their products are used to commit crimes.

Other organizations support gun-control laws. One example is Everytown. This organization gives money to liberal groups and lawmakers.

▲ Wayne LaPierre is the leader of the NRA. His group gives millions of dollars to conservative lawmakers.

Everytown notes that gun companies earn huge profits. At the same time, their products are being used to kill tens of thousands of people every year. Groups such as Everytown want new laws for gun companies. In particular, they want stronger safety standards. They argue that these standards will reduce firearm deaths.

33

CHAPTER 6

DIFFERENT LAWS, DIFFERENT OUTCOMES

Each state has its own gun laws. Some states have few limits on firearms. Other states have many limits. In general, different laws correspond to very different outcomes.

The total number of gun deaths in a state is not always a useful statistic. Large states such as Texas and California have more deaths. But that is because they have more people. For this reason, rates are often a more useful statistic.

Many states make it easy to buy firearms at gun shows.

Rates count the number of gun deaths per 100,000 people. That way, it is easier to compare states of different sizes.

In 2020, Hawaii recorded 3.4 gun deaths per 100,000 people. That was the lowest rate in the country. In contrast, Mississippi recorded 28.6 gun deaths per 100,000 people. That was the highest rate in the country.

Hawaii has some of the strongest gun-control laws in the United States. Mississippi has some of the weakest. This result holds true throughout the country, with few exceptions. States with the strongest gun laws tend to have the lowest rates of gun violence. States with the weakest gun laws tend to have the highest rates.

News reports often focus on shootings in large cities. But gun violence is not limited to urban areas. In fact, rural areas face much higher

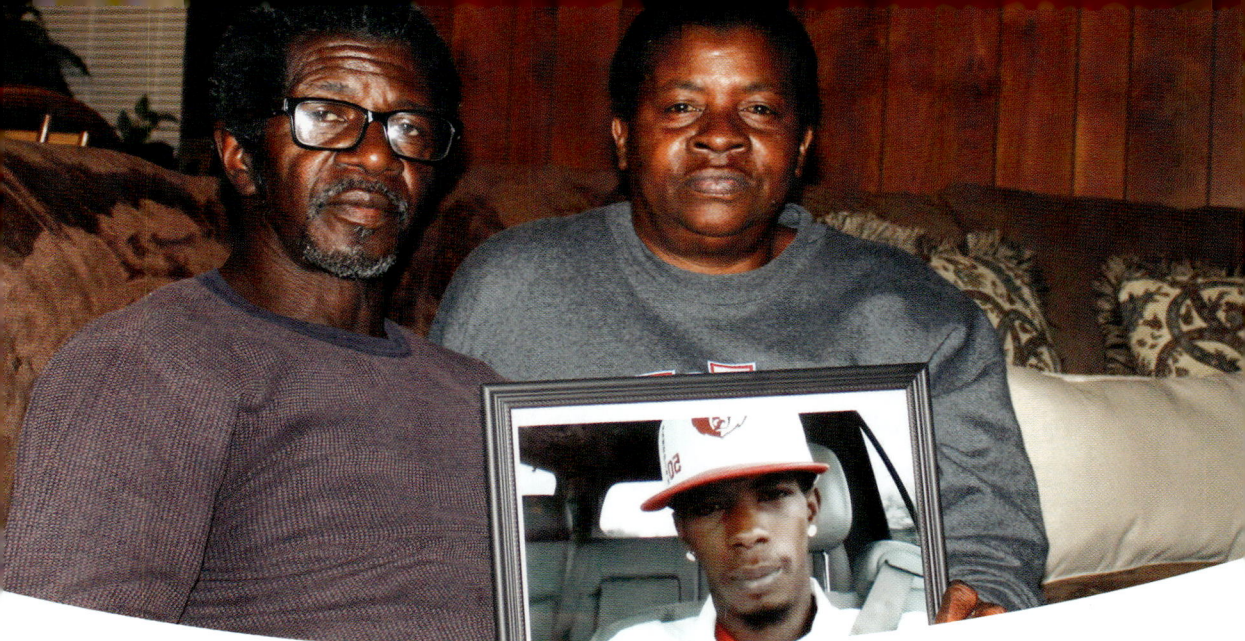

⚠ Two parents in Mississippi hold a picture of their son, who was killed by gun violence.

rates of firearm death. In 2020, rural counties averaged 17 gun deaths per 100,000 people. Large cities averaged 12 deaths per 100,000. However, the type of death depended on the location. Homicides were slightly more common in urban areas. Suicides were far more common in rural areas.

States with weak gun laws typically have high rates of gun ownership. These states also tend to have high suicide rates. For example, Wyoming has some of the weakest gun laws in the country. As of 2020, Wyoming also had the second-highest rate of gun ownership. Meanwhile, the state's firearm suicide rate was 20.9 per 100,000 people. That was the highest rate in the United States.

Likewise, states with strong gun laws typically have low rates of gun ownership. These states also tend to have low suicide rates. For example, New Jersey has some of the strongest gun laws in the country. As of 2020, New Jersey also had the lowest gun-ownership rate. The state's firearm suicide rate was 1.8 per 100,000 people. That was the lowest rate in the United States.

▷ THINK ABOUT IT

Do you think governments have a responsibility to reduce suicide rates? Why or why not?

GUNS AND SUICIDE (2020)

Rate of firearm ownership	Firearm suicides per 100,000 people
1. Montana (66.3%)	1. Wyoming (20.9)
2. Wyoming (66.2%)	2. Alaska (17.8)
3. Alaska (64.5%)	3. Montana (15.8)
4. Idaho (60.1%)	4. Idaho (15.1)
5. West Virginia (58.5%)	5. New Mexico (13.7)
46. New York (19.9%)	46. Rhode Island (2.7)
47. Hawaii (14.9%)	47. Hawaii (2.1)
48. Rhode Island (14.8%)	48. New York (2.1)
49. Massachusetts (14.7%)	49. Massachusetts (1.8)
50. New Jersey (14.7%)	50. New Jersey (1.8)

If you or someone you know is thinking about suicide, call 988 to reach the Suicide & Crisis Lifeline.

CASE STUDY

FIREARM LICENSES

Texas lawmakers debated a new bill in the spring of 2021. It would allow people to carry firearms without a license. Guns could be carried openly, or they could be concealed.

A majority of Texans opposed the bill. Many police departments opposed it, too. They noted that part of the licensing process involves training. It also includes a written test and a shooting test. Without this training, fewer people would be familiar with gun safety. Officers would be at greater risk, they argued. Ordinary citizens would be at greater risk, too.

Conservative lawmakers held different views. They argued that Second Amendment rights were more important than licenses. They also believed the bill would not lead to more crime.

The bill became law in June 2021. As of late 2022, statistics were not yet available for that

▲ Training courses help people learn how to handle firearms safely.

year's rate of gun violence. However, urban police officers had already noticed a difference. They said minor arguments were more likely to lead to gun use. These included disagreements over bad driving, loud music, and parking spots.

Texas was not the only state with such laws. By January 2023, half of US states did not require a license to carry a firearm. For instance, Missouri stopped requiring licenses in 2007. Over the next nine years, Missouri's firearm homicide rate increased by 47 percent.

CHAPTER 7

FINDING COMMON GROUND

Americans' opinions on guns depend on a variety of factors. Race is one. A 2021 poll asked Americans about gun violence. Eight in ten Black Americans saw gun violence as a major problem. But only four in ten white Americans saw it as a problem. Political views also affect attitudes. The same poll showed that eight in ten conservatives opposed stronger gun laws. But eight in ten liberals supported stronger gun laws.

Approximately four in ten Americans live in a home with a gun.

Location matters, too. In rural areas, most people oppose stronger laws. But in urban areas, most people support stronger laws.

Despite the debates, a majority of Americans agree on certain gun laws. One type of law requires background checks for all gun buyers. Another law allows states to deny concealed-carry licenses. A third type prevents people from buying guns if they have been convicted of a violent crime. Studies show that each of these laws reduces firearm homicide rates. Homicide rates tend to be lowest when all three laws are in effect at the same time. However, many states do not have any of these three laws.

A majority of gun owners also support stronger gun-control laws. But most gun owners believe people who don't own guns view them as part of the problem. Owners also tend to think

▲ In 2019, New York passed a "red flag" law. It lets police take guns from people who threaten themselves or others.

non-owners want to take away all guns. For this reason, gun owners who support gun-control laws are unlikely to talk about their views.

Researchers urge respectful conversation between gun owners and non-owners. They also urge non-owners to acknowledge that people have a right to own firearms. That way, the topic can become less political. Researchers say if this happens, stronger laws will be more likely to make their way through Congress.

FOCUS ON
GUN LAWS IN AMERICA

Write your answers on a separate piece of paper.

1. Write a paragraph that explains the main ideas of Chapter 6.

2. Do you agree with the Supreme Court's 2008 ruling that the Second Amendment applies to all individuals? Why or why not?

3. Which state had the lowest rate of gun violence in 2020?
    - A. Texas
    - B. Hawaii
    - C. Wyoming

4. If a state has weak gun-control laws, which is most likely to be true?
    - A. The state has a low rate of firearm ownership.
    - B. The state has a high rate of background checks.
    - C. The state has a high rate of firearm suicide.

Answer key on page 48.

GLOSSARY

amendments
Official changes to a document.

appealed
Asked a higher court to review a case.

background checks
Reports on people's criminal, financial, and other history.

concealed
Hidden from view.

conservative
Supporting traditional views or values, often resisting changes.

domestic violence
Abuse that someone commits against a person in his or her household.

federal
Having to do with the top level of government, involving the whole nation rather than just one state.

homicide
The killing of one person by another person.

liberal
Supporting changes to traditional views or values.

lobbying
Trying to affect the decisions of lawmakers.

register
To make a record on an official list.

TO LEARN MORE

BOOKS

Doeden, Matt. *Gun Violence: Fighting for Our Lives and Our Rights*. Minneapolis: Lerner Publishing, 2020.

Harris, Duchess, with Jennifer Simms. *Mass Shootings in America*. Minneapolis: Abdo Publishing, 2019.

Rowell, Rebecca. *Parkland Students Challenge the National Rifle Association*. Lake Elmo, MN: Focus Readers, 2019.

NOTE TO EDUCATORS

Visit **www.focusreaders.com** to find lesson plans, activities, links, and other resources related to this title.

INDEX

background checks, 7, 44
Biden, Joe, 7
Black Americans, 12, 17, 25, 30, 43
Black Panther Party, 16–17
Buffalo, New York, 5, 7

crime, 15, 18, 21, 30–31, 32, 40, 44

domestic violence, 25–26

Everytown, 32–33

Federal Assault Weapons Ban, 18–19

Heller, Dick Anthony, 20

licenses, 17–18, 20, 40–41, 44

mass shootings, 5–6, 18–19, 26
militias, 9–11, 16, 20

Miller, Jack, 16

National Rifle Association, 32

Second Amendment, 11–12, 16, 20, 40
self-defense, 9, 20, 29
suicide, 26–27, 37–39

Uvalde, Texas, 5, 7

Washington, DC, 20

Answer Key: 1. Answers will vary; 2. Answers will vary; 3. B; 4. C